The Money Mindset

Reshaping Your Mind about
Psychology of Money and Insightful
lessons on managing wealth and
finding happiness

By

Lane J. Taylor

The Money Mindset

Disclaimer

The content presented in this book is intended for informational and educational purposes only. The author, Lane J. Taylor, is not a financial advisor, and the strategies, insights, and recommendations offered in this book should not be considered as professional financial, legal, or business advice.

Readers are encouraged to seek the advice of qualified professionals for personalized guidance pertaining to their individual situations. The author and publisher make no representations or warranties regarding the accuracy, completeness, or suitability of the information provided. The use of any information from this book is at the reader's own discretion and risk.

The author and publisher disclaim any liability for any direct, indirect, incidental, consequential, or special damages arising out of or in any way connected with the use of this book or the information presented within. It is essential for readers to independently verify and assess the applicability of the strategies outlined in this book based on their specific circumstances.

The mention of specific products, services, or third-party websites does not constitute an endorsement or recommendation. The author has made reasonable efforts to ensure the accuracy of the information at the time of writing, but technological advancements and changes may have occurred since then.

The author is not affiliated with any third-party products or services mentioned in this book, and any references are provided for illustrative purposes only. The success of any strategies or techniques depends on various factors, and individual results may vary.

By reading this book, the reader acknowledges and agrees to the terms of this disclaimer. It is recommended to consult with appropriate professionals before making any significant decisions based on the information presented in this book.

About the author

Lane J. Taylor is a distinguished financial expert and dedicated researcher known for his expertise in wealth-building principles and financial markets. Beyond traditional finance, he delves into the intersection of finance and technology, offering forward-thinking insights. Committed to demystifying financial concepts, Taylor's research applies real-world applications for accessible wealth-building. As a sought-after speaker, he shares actionable insights on investment strategies, technology, and the psychology of wealth. Taylor remains at the forefront of financial and technological advancements, inspiring others to explore the potential at the intersection of finance and technology for financial prosperity.

Table of contents

The Money Mindset

Introduction

"In a vibrant city, there resided a young man named Oliver, born into affluence. Endowed with ample financial resources, he reveled in a lavish and extravagant lifestyle. Despite his intelligence and sharp wit, Oliver's wealth appeared to insulate him from the teachings of humility and responsible conduct.

Over time, Oliver's approach to finances grew progressively careless. He indulged in extravagant parties, lavish acquisitions, and risky investments, fueled by a confidence in his intellect that obscured the necessity of humility and prudent financial behavior.

Amidst his extravagant way of life, there was one evening that remained vivid in Oliver's mind. Among a group of admirers at an upscale club, he impulsively made a striking gesture. Ordering a fine bottle of Hennessy, he raised it high for all to witness before unexpectedly pouring its contents onto his pricey wristwatch. The room fell silent, the extravagance of the act leaving behind an enduring impression of opulence verging on imprudence.

Another example highlighted Oliver's quest for superficial status. Motivated by the urge to impress people who scarcely knew him, he indulged in a shopping binge, acquiring items he neither required nor genuinely appreciated. His wardrobe brimmed with designer attire, his residence adorned with superfluous luxuries. Unbeknownst to him, these shallow exhibitions amounted to hollow triumphs, merely crafting a facade of affluence.

The Hennessy incident and the spree of extravagant shopping were not singular occurrences but rather manifestations of a more profound problem – Oliver's distorted perception of wealth and his relentless urge to seek approval from others. These indulgences, motivated by a craving for external validation, represented the weaknesses in the framework of his financial security.

The pivotal moment arrived when the volatile market took a downturn, causing Oliver's investments to collapse and his previously thriving business empire to confront the stark truth of insolvency. The riches that had characterized his identity were slipping through his fingers, laying bare the vulnerabilities he had overlooked.

Following his financial collapse, Oliver underwent a period of introspection, contemplating the genuine essence of success and prosperity. He came to understand that while conventional attributes like intelligence and acumen held merit, they alone were insufficient to ensure financial security. It was his conduct, characterized by arrogance and a deficiency of humility, that had played a significant role in his downfall."

Welcome to the preface of "The Money Mindset." Within these initial pages, our goal is to reshape your outlook on financial achievement. Unlike the traditional notion that intelligence is the sole determinant of financial prowess, this book contends that true mastery involves various elements such as behavior, conscientious spending, and more.

As you begin this voyage, be ready to uncover the profound revelation that intellect and cleverness play a small part in effective money management. Instead, the focus shifts to the frequently underestimated yet highly influential element—your behavior. This introduction lays the groundwork for a more profound investigation, offering perspectives into the intricate correlation between behavior and financial well-being.

Prepare to challenge conventional wisdom, interrogate presumptions, and adopt a fresh perspective on prosperity. Subsequent chapters will explore the intricate mechanisms through which behavior molds financial trajectories. Therefore, unlock your mind, absorb the forthcoming teachings, and commence the journey of metamorphosis.

Chapter 1

Peril or Fortuity

Luck, frequently overlooked and misinterpreted, subtly but undeniably contributes to the fabric of financial achievement. While many contend that careful planning, strategic choices, and diligence alone dictate prosperity, recognizing the impact of luck is essential for a thorough understanding of one's financial path.

Luck in finance transcends mere chance; it involves a multifaceted interaction of unforeseen occurrences and situations that can either elevate an individual to remarkable achievements or present unforeseen obstacles. To delve deeper into this idea, let's examine a fictional narrative that illustrates the intricate influence of luck on financial prosperity.

Consider the below narrative:

"Introducing Alex, a conscientious worker whose ascent up the corporate hierarchy embodies the traits typically linked with achievement: diligence, commitment, and proficiency. Years spent refining skills within a secure sector had provided a bedrock of stability, but Alex's financial path took an unforeseen turn, highlighting the pivotal influence of luck.

During a typical networking event one evening, Alex engaged in conversation with a forward-thinking entrepreneur venturing into unexplored territories. This seemingly chance encounter laid the groundwork for a career shift that, in the moment, felt almost fateful. The fresh endeavor not only matched Alex's capabilities but also offered prospects that surpassed the boundaries of meticulous preparation.

The venture flourished, catapulting Alex to unprecedented levels of financial prosperity. The unexpected encounter at the networking event emerged as a pivotal juncture that challenged traditional narratives of success tied solely to one's professional trajectory. In this scenario, luck served as the driving force that magnified Alex's endeavors and situated them within a realm of unexpected possibilities."

Alex's narrative underscores the delicate interplay between our intentions and the unforeseen turns of fate, where an apparently arbitrary encounter can alter the entire trajectory of financial success. It serves as a poignant reminder that, despite living in a world where strategic planning and professional skills frequently take center stage, luck remains an unpredictable influence capable of reshaping our financial paths.

In the domain of financial achievement, luck transcends simple chance; it encompasses a intricate interaction of unexpected occurrences and situations. Recognizing this dynamic relationship cultivates humility amidst success, prompting individuals to acknowledge the unpredictable aspects of their financial trajectories.

Taking a broader view of the overarching tale of financial triumph, recognizing luck as a multifaceted influencer prompts a more nuanced outlook. It doesn't diminish the significance of diligence, strategic choices, and expertise. Rather, it invites individuals to traverse the financial terrain with a mix of resilience, flexibility, and a recognition of the unpredictable interplay between destiny and financial prosperity. Ultimately, in the human saga of affluence and achievement, each twist of fate, every happenstance encounter, contributes layers to the narrative, rendering it distinctly ours to navigate and cherish.

A Key to Smart Money Management

Safeguarding against risks in finance parallels guiding a ship through turbulent seas, demanding a nuanced blend of strategy, foresight, and flexibility. This constitutes a cornerstone of astute financial stewardship, often distinguishing those who prosper from those who face challenges in the financial arena. Let's unravel the intricacies of this vital skill, leveraging real-life examples to highlight its practical importance.

Picture beginning a financial voyage as a person named Alex, evaluating the inherent risks associated with investments, market shifts, and unexpected events. Understanding that risk is an inherent aspect of the financial terrain, Alex realizes that the goal isn't to eradicate risks entirely but to maneuver through them strategically.

Risk tolerance, a profoundly individual measure, significantly influences Alex's path. Analogous to a ship's captain evaluating the vessel's ability to withstand rough seas, individuals must determine their capacity to endure financial volatility without succumbing to rash choices. With a high risk tolerance, Alex might pursue ventures promising substantial returns, whereas someone like Emily, with a lower risk tolerance, prioritizes stability over the allure of risky investments, particularly as they approach later stages of life.

Diversification emerges as a vital instrument in the financial navigator's toolkit, resembling the wisdom of not placing all assets in one investment. Jack and Emma's experiences exemplify this concept. While Jack concentrates his investments heavily in a single industry, leaving him vulnerable to substantial losses if it falters, Emma diversifies her portfolio across multiple sectors. In the event of one sector underperforming, Emma's diversified approach mitigates the full impact, demonstrating how spreading risks can be a prudent strategy.

Entrepreneurs, such as Sarah, navigating the business landscape, must excel in risk management to ensure enduring success. Sarah's careful preparation, recognition of potential obstacles, and execution of backup strategies exemplify the fluidity of risk in entrepreneurship. Her diversified methods for acquiring clients and generating revenue strengthen her business resilience against unexpected hurdles.

Emergency funds serve as financial safety nets, offering protection against unforeseen crises. James, armed with such a fund, adeptly manages a sudden job loss without turning to high-interest debt. This financial cushion provides reassurance, enabling individuals to navigate unexpected challenges without compromising their long-term financial objectives.

Insurance emerges as a potent tool in mitigating risks. Maria's situation, where property insurance proves invaluable following a natural calamity, highlights the protective function insurance serves in financial preparation. Despite requiring regular premiums, the security it provides during unexpected adversities often surpasses the associated costs.

In the constantly changing financial environment, continual learning and adjustment are essential. Effective money management demands a dedication to ongoing learning, enabling individuals to make well-informed choices amidst shifting conditions.

As we traverse the uncertain terrain of finance, accepting risk as a controllable factor empowers us to make educated decisions, adjust to shifting circumstances, and establish a resilient and prosperous financial path.

Strategy for Long-Term Prosperity

In the quest for lasting prosperity, a nuanced interplay between luck and strategy takes center stage. Recognizing the influence of luck, with its unforeseeable turns of fate, is fundamental. Meanwhile, strategy acts as the steadfast ally, offering a blueprint for enduring achievement.

This intricate balance necessitates a nuanced comprehension, devoid of the belief that either element must dominate the other.

Luck introduces an element of uncertainty, wherein serendipitous meetings or unexpected hurdles can profoundly shape the path of financial endeavors. It's a factor beyond complete manipulation but demands acknowledgment and, when feasible, utilization. However, relying solely on luck is not a viable method for enduring wealth.

Strategy, resembling the North Star, embodies the deliberate and reflective preparation essential for financial triumph. It encompasses careful objective establishment, measured decision-making, and flexibility in the face of alterations. Employing a strategic mindset enables individuals and enterprises to navigate ambiguities and seize chances, furnishing a sturdy groundwork for advancement.

The harmony between luck and strategy represents the optimal zone for sustained prosperity. It's not a matter of choosing one over the other but rather recognizing that both can harmoniously coexist and enhance each other. While strategy offers a structured blueprint, luck can act as a catalyst, elevating endeavors to unexpected levels. The strategic-minded individual positions themselves to capitalize on serendipitous opportunities that align with their overarching objectives.

Flexibility emerges as a foundational characteristic in navigating this intricate equilibrium. Unanticipated occurrences, whether influenced by luck or external factors, call for a swift and agile response. Inflexibility risks stagnation, whereas adaptability enables the adjustment of tactics to harmonize with evolving circumstances. It's the capacity to transform unforeseen challenges into opportunities and to pivot when the terrain unexpectedly shifts.

Fostering a mindset of continual enhancement further bolsters the pursuit of enduring prosperity. Drawing lessons from experiences, honing strategies, and staying abreast of emerging trends are vital components. A dedication to growth and flexibility ensures that the approach remains dynamic and adaptable to the perpetually evolving financial landscape.

Fundamentally, the quest for lasting prosperity entails a seamless integration of luck and strategy. Acknowledging the impact of luck while not depending entirely on it, strategic foresight acts as the cornerstone, furnishing stability and guidance. The synergy between these elements facilitates the augmentation of achievements, with adaptability and ongoing enhancement serving as drivers for continual expansion. This nuanced comprehension of the interplay between luck and strategy constructs a resilient narrative within the intricate realm of finance, steering the path toward enduring prosperity.

The Money Mindset

Chapter 2

Insatiable

In the relentless drive for financial achievement, the deceptive notion of "Never Enough" can loom large, skewing perspectives and diverting individuals from satisfaction. This misleading mindset, fueled by an incessant desire for more, frequently results in an endless cycle of dissatisfaction and lack of fulfillment. Unpacking the complexities of this illusion necessitates a thorough examination of its roots, manifestations, and the transformative potential of nurturing a mindset grounded in contentment. Essentially, the illusion of "Never Enough" originates from societal narratives and external pressures that reinforce the notion that greater accumulation equates to triumph and contentment. The incessant stream of messages advocating for increased possessions, heightened wealth, and elevated status can cultivate a mentality where contentment remains elusive, constantly overshadowed by an unquenchable thirst for further riches and belongings.

This deception materializes across different domains, spanning personal finances to career ambitions. People may constantly pursue financial objectives, convinced that attaining a particular income level or amassing a certain wealth will ultimately fulfill their quest for achievement. Yet, the evasive concept of "Enough" becomes evident in this scenario as fresh standards consistently arise, shifting the goalposts farther beyond reach.

Within consumerism, the illusion of "Never Enough" is epitomized by the continual chase for material goods. The longing for the newest gadgets, most fashionable attire, or larger residences evolves into an endless pursuit, driven by the belief that obtaining more will enhance one's social standing or provide enduring contentment. However, the fleeting nature of these pleasures ensnares individuals in an unending cycle of desire.

In the realm of career aspirations, the illusion of "Never Enough" exerts its influence as well. Driven by societal norms and the quest for achievement, ambitious individuals may discover themselves caught in a perpetual cycle of striving. Ascending the professional hierarchy, amassing recognition, and accruing wealth can lose their significance when pursued under the belief that each milestone is merely a precursor to the next, with satisfaction never truly attained.

Escaping the grip of the "Never Enough" illusion demands a shift in perspective—one that transcends external indicators of success and redirects attention towards internal values and contentment. This evolution entails nurturing a mindset of sufficiency, where individuals acknowledge and value their current possessions, understanding that genuine abundance surpasses material wealth.

Embracing sufficiency requires a deliberate cultivation of gratitude—a recognition of the present and an appreciation for the resources, relationships, and opportunities already present in one's life. This intentional change in focus serves as a potent remedy to the ceaseless desire for more, fostering a sense of fulfillment rooted in the richness of the present moment.

Moreover, striving for a purpose-driven existence can serve as an antidote to the "Never

Enough" illusion. By aligning their endeavors with core values and actively contributing to meaningful causes, individuals experience a deep sense of fulfillment. Pursuing a purpose that transcends mere material gain offers authentic satisfaction and dispels the misconception that fulfillment hinges on external measures of success.

Engaging in financial mindfulness plays a vital role in deconstructing the "Never Enough" illusion. It entails being mindful of one's financial choices, distinguishing between necessities and desires, and making deliberate decisions that reflect personal values. Budgeting, saving, and investing with a focus on sufficiency rather than abundance foster a more balanced and constructive approach to managing finances. An exploration of societal narratives and the cultural celebration of excess can assist in dispelling the illusion of "Never Enough." By scrutinizing prevailing norms and redefining personal interpretations of success, individuals can liberate themselves from the relentless pursuit of accumulation. This involves embracing the notion that success extends beyond external benchmarks and is, instead, a deeply individual and subjective concept.

Ultimately, the illusion of "Never Enough" can be deconstructed through deliberate and mindful shifts in perspective. By embracing sufficiency, practicing gratitude, pursuing purpose, fostering financial mindfulness, and challenging societal narratives, individuals can break free from the cycle of perpetual desire. In doing so, they come to realize that genuine prosperity is not found in ceaseless acquisition but in the profound acknowledgment that, in the present moment, they possess "Enough."

Breaking Free from the Consumerism Trap

In today's contemporary society, it's effortless to become entangled in the ceaseless quest for greater—more belongings, more adventures, more of everything. This continuous pursuit, commonly known as the Consumerism Trap, suggests that happiness lies in amassing possessions. However, the outcome often leaves us with a peculiar sense of emptiness, as though the pursuit of more has fallen short in filling the void.

This consumer-driven culture isn't a recent phenomenon; its roots can be traced back to the post-World War II era, a time marked by economic prosperity. The transition from wartime economies to ones centered around consumption laid the groundwork for the emergence of consumerism as we recognize it today. Advertisers became increasingly adept at persuading us that our happiness and success depended on our next significant purchase.

The Consumerism Trap manifests in various ways, with one notable aspect being our disposable culture. We are incessantly bombarded with advertisements for newer, shinier products, which diminishes the appeal of our current possessions. This mentality of planned obsolescence not only contributes to environmental issues but also perpetuates a cycle of dissatisfaction, as we are constantly seeking the next upgrade.

Next comes the comparison game, a challenging mental landscape where we gauge our success and contentment against the carefully curated lives of others, particularly on social media platforms. It becomes an endless cycle of comparison, frequently leading to feelings of inadequacy and the misconception that everyone else's life is somehow more gratifying.

Breaking free from the Consumerism Trap requires a shift in mindset. It entails acknowledging that seeking happiness primarily through material possessions is akin to chasing an elusive dream. One must question societal standards and redefine personal values, realizing that genuine fulfillment extends far beyond mere ownership of material goods.

Practicing mindful consumption can revolutionize your approach to purchasing. It involves being deliberate in your buying decisions, discerning between necessities and desires, and opting for items that resonate with your values. Minimalism often comes into play, prioritizing quality over quantity and cultivating a life free from unnecessary clutter.

Financial mindfulness is also crucial in this equation. It entails recognizing your spending patterns, establishing a budget that mirrors your values, and making choices that propel you toward your financial objectives. Transitioning from thoughtless consumption to purposeful spending can be empowering.

Redirecting attention from material goods to experiences represents a profound shift. Experiences, whether through travel, relationships, or personal development, often yield deeper satisfaction compared to the temporary gratification of owning possessions. Investing in experiences is an investment in a more fulfilling and meaningful life.

Engaging with the community and sharing experiences serve as potent remedies for the Consumerism Trap. By connecting with others, participating in communal endeavors, and working toward shared objectives, the emphasis transitions from individualism to collective well-being. This sense of community fosters a richer and more enduring source of fulfillment.

Education and awareness are integral in escaping the Consumerism Trap. Recognizing the psychological tactics employed in marketing, grasping the environmental ramifications of consumerism, and comprehending the outcomes of unrestrained consumption empower individuals to make enlightened decisions.

Sustainability emerges as a central tenet in breaking away from consumerist patterns. Choosing products designed for durability, endorsing environmentally conscious brands, and reducing waste are steps toward cultivating a more mindful and ecologically sustainable way of life.

Escaping the Consumerism Trap isn't about forsaking modern conveniences; rather, it's about deliberately selecting a lifestyle that resonates with your core beliefs. It entails embarking on a path of self-exploration, questioning conventional expectations, and placing emphasis on authenticity and genuine fulfillment.

Contentment as a Path to Sustainable Wealth

Amidst the ceaseless pursuit of wealth, there exists a compelling alternative: embracing contentment. This sustainable approach to prosperity isn't rooted in perpetual desires for more; rather, it involves discovering satisfaction in one's current possessions and circumstances. It entails adopting a mindset that prioritizes personal well-being, living with awareness, and cherishing the abundance found in the present instant, transcending the incessant quest for external symbols of achievement.

Fostering contentment entails embracing life's modest joys, nurturing meaningful connections, and finding purpose beyond material acquisitions. It marks a divergence from societal norms that equate happiness solely with amassing riches and belongings. This perspective views wealth through a holistic lens, encompassing not only financial assets but also physical, mental, and emotional wellness.

The journey commences with a change in outlook, requiring a deliberate choice to refrain from incessant comparison and societal expectations regarding materialism. Recognizing the wealth already existing in one's life serves as the impetus for this change. Mindful living is pivotal, promoting purposeful attention to the present and fostering a deeper engagement with life's moments.

Delving into your core values and priorities stands as another crucial facet of this voyage. Harmonizing daily decisions with these values steers choices, fostering a more deliberate and enriching trajectory in life. Interconnection and communal bonds hold significance – meaningful connections substantially contribute to a sense of fulfillment. The richness of a supportive community transcends mere financial metrics.

In the pursuit of sustainable wealth through contentment, financial decisions acquire a fresh perspective. Choices are steered by a sense of satisfaction and conscientious distribution of resources. Financial objectives harmonize with individual values, pivoting the focus from amassing possessions to crafting a life imbued with genuineness and purpose.

The profound influence of nurturing contentment becomes apparent in its effect on mental and emotional health. As individuals let go of the constant pursuit of more, stress dissipates, giving rise to a profound inner calm. This mental fortitude serves as a valuable resource, enhancing the enduring stability of wealth amidst life's unavoidable trials.

Ultimately, fostering contentment presents a profound and enduring route to prosperity. It counters the traditional belief associating happiness solely with outward accomplishments and acquisitions. Rather, it redirects attention to the richness inherent in one's current circumstances, nurturing a mindset of satisfaction and appreciation. Sustainable wealth, rooted in contentment, embraces comprehensive well-being, deliberate living, and the authentic pursuit of values-aligned objectives. This purposeful quest for contentment not only reshapes individual experiences but also fosters the development of a stronger and more fulfilled community.

Chapter 3

Complex Amplification

Within the domain of financial strategies, few ideas hold as significant sway and promise as the phenomenon of compounding. Revered as the "eighth wonder of the world" by Albert Einstein, this force stands as a remarkable mechanism capable of propelling individuals towards enduring financial well-being. Grasping and adeptly leveraging the power of compounding isn't merely a financial acumen; it serves as a crucial tool for unlocking considerable growth and accumulating wealth over the long haul.

At its essence, compounding involves the growth of an investment not only on the initial principal but also on the accrued interest or returns from earlier periods. What sets compounding apart is its exponential characteristic: as the investment expands, the generated returns also contribute to its overall growth, creating a compounding effect that magnifies over time.

The enchantment of compounding lies in the concept of earning returns not only on the initial investment but also on the returns accumulated from prior periods. This compounding phenomenon has the potential to turn even modest contributions into substantial wealth over a prolonged duration. Initiating investments early allows for more time for compounding to take effect, thereby enhancing its impact.

Consider two scenarios: one where an individual invests a lump sum amount at the age of 25 and another where someone begins investing the same amount annually from the age of 35. Despite contributing the same total amount by the age of 65, the individual who initiated investments earlier would likely possess a considerably larger portfolio due to the additional years of compounding.

Harnessing the power of compounding commences with understanding the critical role of time. The sooner one begins investing, the more time the investment has to grow exponentially. Hence, financial advisors often emphasize the importance of commencing investments as early as possible. Whether it involves utilizing a retirement account, mutual funds, or other investment avenues, the key lies in initiating the compounding process and allowing time to facilitate its growth.

Maintaining consistency is another fundamental aspect of effective compounding. Regularly contributing to investments, even with modest amounts, can result in significant growth over time. The steadfastness in contributions ensures a continuous influx of funds to compound, further enhancing the overall impact. It's the financial discipline of consistently investing, irrespective of market fluctuations, that sets apart those who leverage compounding effectively.

Reinvesting returns is a critical tactic in compounding. Instead of withdrawing the returns generated by an investment, allowing them to be reinvested and contribute to the principal amount accelerates the compounding process. This approach capitalizes on the compounding effect not only on the initial investment but also on the increasing returns, facilitating exponential growth.

Diversification serves as a protective mechanism in leveraging the potential of compounding. By spreading investments across various assets or sectors, risks can be mitigated, and the overall portfolio can be safeguarded. While compounding yields substantial growth, it remains susceptible to market fluctuations. Diversification aids in risk management, ensuring the continuity of the compounding process over the long term.

Understanding the essence of compounding entails grasping the concept of the compounding period. This period refers to the frequency at which interest is added to the principal amount. The frequency of compounding significantly influences overall growth. Whether interest compounds annually, quarterly, or monthly can profoundly affect the final accumulated amount. Hence, opting for investments with more frequent compounding can augment the efficacy of this financial strategy.

The reinvestment of dividends presents another layer of compounding. Investments that yield dividends, like stocks, provide the opportunity to reinvest those dividends back into the investment. This not only compounds the initial capital but also amplifies the income generated by the investment, leading to a more rapid growth trajectory.

While compounding offers significant benefits, it's crucial to consider fees and taxes. High fees can eat into the returns generated by compounding, diminishing its overall impact. Similarly, understanding the tax implications of various investment strategies ensures individuals can optimize their after-tax returns, thereby maximizing the compounding process.

The power of compounding extends beyond traditional investments; it can also be applied to debt reduction. By expediting the repayment of debts such as loans or mortgages, individuals can save on interest payments, which can then be redirected towards investments. This dual strategy—reducing debts while simultaneously investing—leverages compounding in both directions, bolstering overall financial health.

Pitfalls of Ignoring Compounding in Investment Strategies

In the realm of finance, compounding functions as a hidden ingredient for wealth creation, yet overlooking its importance can lead to significant pitfalls. Analogous to baking a cake, forgetting this crucial component diminishes the final outcome's delight. Likewise, postponing the commencement of investments resembles procrastinating on adding the secret sauce. Even a brief delay markedly diminishes the potential for exponential growth of your assets over time. Consistency is paramount; it entails regularly incorporating a dash of that secret sauce.

Skipping contributions or occasional fund withdrawals disrupt the continuity and restrict the enchantment that compounding can unleash.

Now, let's delve into withdrawals. Picture this scenario: you're saving up for a significant goal, such as a dream vacation. However, you intermittently dip into your savings. It's akin to sipping from your secret sauce intermittently—an inadvisable move. Compounding thrives when returns are reinvested, fostering a snowball effect. Frequent withdrawals not only impede this magical progression but also deplete the reservoir of sauce available to work its wonders. Moreover, be wary of fees! They resemble stealthy gremlins capable of devouring your secret sauce. High fees nibble away at your returns, diminishing the potency of the compounding effect.

Understanding compounding periods is akin to knowing the optimal baking time for a cake—it's crucial. Disregarding these periods or lacking awareness of how frequently interest accrues can disrupt the entire recipe. And let's not overlook dividends—they're akin to additional spices that can enhance your cake's flavor profile. Reinvesting dividends enables your secret sauce to work not only on the initial investment but also on the supplementary taste they bring.

Now, consider returns. It's not solely about the amount you earn; it's about what you can actually purchase with it. Neglecting the impact of inflation is akin to overlooking the fact that prices continually rise. If your returns fail to outpace inflation, you might end up with a seemingly substantial cake that lacks sweetness. Lastly, employing compounding to address debts resembles multitasking in the kitchen—simultaneously paying off debts and investing. It's a savvy maneuver that adds an additional dimension to your financial recipe.

To steer clear of these traps, view compounding as your key ingredient for financial triumph. Kick things off early, maintain a steady contribution, allow returns to reinvest, watch out for hidden fees, grasp compounding intervals, enhance your strategy with dividends, and leverage compounding to address debts. When you nail down these elements, you're not merely baking a cake; you're crafting a masterpiece of enduring and resilient wealth accumulation.

Maximizing Returns

Imagine your financial journey as tending to a garden, with compounding serving as the enchanted soil that transforms your endeavors into a thriving oasis. To harness this enchantment fully, sow your financial seeds early – time acts as sunlight for your investments. Maintain a consistent watering routine by contributing regularly; it's not about grand gestures but the dependable rhythm that allows compounding to weave its magic. View your returns as seeds too; refrain from plucking them out but instead let them sprout into a compounding snowball. Strategically diversify your garden to withstand various market seasons, and remember to occasionally trim and adjust as your financial landscape evolves. Employ tax-efficient strategies as nourishment, align your garden with long-term goals, and keep a vigilant eye on sneaky fees – they're akin to weeds that can impede growth. Stay curious and informed, educate yourself about financial flora, and periodically assess if your risk tolerance aligns with your garden's temperament.

These strategies serve as your compasses, guiding you through the financial terrain, maximizing returns, and cultivating a resilient path to enduring prosperity.

Chapter 4

Accumulating and Maintaining Wealth

"Allow me to introduce Jake, a young man with a discerning vision for financial craftsmanship. From the outset, he grasped that building wealth wasn't merely a short sprint but rather a meticulously planned marathon. Jake's initial stroke on this canvas was the prompt commencement of his journey. Straight out of college, he began investing a portion of his earnings, recognizing that time stood as his most valuable asset.

Consistency became Jake's chosen spectrum. Each month, unwaveringly, he contributed to his investment portfolio. It wasn't about making grand gestures but rather maintaining a steadfast cadence, crafting a financial palette characterized by endurance and steadfastness.

As Jake's investments began yielding results, he adeptly employed the strategy of reinvesting returns. Instead of cashing out his gains, he allowed them to compound, adding new layers to his financial canvas. Each reinvested gain contributed to the intricate texture of his wealth portrait, enriching its overall complexity.

Diversification served as Jake's method of equilibrium. Recognizing the significance of spreading risk, he prudently diversified his portfolio across various assets. This approach resembled an artist meticulously selecting colors to compose a harmonious painting – Jake curated a resilient and well-balanced financial masterpiece.

Regular review and adjustment embodied Jake's curator's expertise. He didn't simply set his investments and leave them untouched; rather, he periodically stepped back to evaluate and refine. This practice ensured that his financial composition remained aligned with his evolving objectives and the dynamic economic landscape.

Jake employed tax-efficient strategies as his nuanced shading. Understanding that taxes could dull the brilliance of his financial masterpiece, he utilized tax-advantaged accounts and carefully considered the tax ramifications of his actions, enhancing the sophistication of his wealth creation.

Aligning his investments with long-term objectives became the overarching motif in Jake's financial tale. He embraced a central theme that directed his artistic decisions, crafting a coherent and meaningful wealth narrative.

Monitoring and reducing fees served as Jake's tools of precision. Similar to an artist valuing the quality of materials, Jake was attentive to fees, ensuring that his financial composition remained pristine and unaffected.

Remaining informed and educated served as Jake's ongoing study of technique. He engaged in the financial equivalent of attending art classes, staying abreast of market trends and strategies, honing his financial acumen.

Periodically reassessing his risk tolerance introduced adaptability into Jake's artistic process. He acknowledged that his preferences and circumstances might evolve, allowing for a flexible and responsive approach to his financial journey.

The culmination of Jake's artistic endeavor wasn't merely wealth accumulation; it was a financial masterpiece that endured the passage of time. His wealth stood as a testament to the artistry of his strategic and deliberate financial decisions. Ultimately, Jake didn't just amass wealth; he crafted a financial legacy that mirrored the artistry of a well-lived and purposeful financial existence."

Challenges in Sustaining Wealth

Preserving wealth entails navigating a path riddled with challenges, each demanding a methodical approach to protect the rewards of diligence and financial achievement. One prevalent obstacle is the temptation of lifestyle inflation. With increasing incomes, there arises a natural inclination to elevate spending patterns, jeopardizing the ability to sustain wealth in the long run. It's a delicate equilibrium that necessitates deliberate choices to enhance lifestyle while upholding financial prudence.

Another hazard is the oversight of risk management. Safeguarding wealth entails readiness for unforeseen circumstances, yet many underestimate the significance of insurance coverage and emergency funds. Neglecting to reinforce these defenses exposes wealth to unexpected downturns or emergencies. Mismanagement of investments poses a substantial risk as well. Poor decisions, a lack of diversification, or the pursuit of short-term gains can swiftly deplete wealth. Regularly reassessing investment portfolios, staying abreast of developments, and seeking professional guidance are essential to circumvent this peril.

Tax inefficiency poses a frequently underestimated challenge. Insufficient tax planning can result in unnecessary financial losses. Utilizing proactive tax strategies, such as leveraging tax-efficient investment vehicles, is imperative for effectively preserving wealth.

Inadequate estate planning presents another potential hazard. Without a well-devised plan, the smooth transition of wealth to the next generation may be compromised, inviting potential disputes, complexities, or tax liabilities. Addressing this challenge entails crafting an estate plan that aligns with personal objectives and legal requirements.

A deficiency in ongoing financial education can impede the maintenance of wealth. Economic landscapes evolve, and remaining static in financial knowledge may lead to outdated strategies. Regularly updating financial literacy ensures the capacity to adapt to changing circumstances and make well-informed decisions.

Relying too heavily on a single income source presents a precarious challenge. Dependence on one source of income heightens vulnerability to economic fluctuations or industry-specific downturns. Diversifying income streams enhances resilience, thereby mitigating this risk.

Underestimating the importance of health and well-being poses another significant threat to the sustainability of wealth. Health issues can incur substantial expenses, impacting financial stability. Prioritizing physical and mental well-being contributes to long-term wealth sustainability by reducing potential healthcare-related financial burdens.

Lastly, inadequate communication and transparency within family structures can have detrimental effects. Failing to openly discuss financial matters, including wealth management strategies and inheritance plans, can lead to misunderstandings or conflicts. Establishing clear communication channels promotes a shared understanding of financial objectives and ensures a unified approach to maintaining wealth across generations.

Building a Lasting Legacy

Embarking on the journey to create a lasting legacy goes beyond mere wealth accumulation; it demands a strategic approach to preserve and transfer financial prosperity through generations. Consider the Johnson family, whose patriarch prioritized financial education during family gatherings. By fostering a culture of understanding in responsible financial management, investments, and the core values underpinning their wealth, the Johnsons nurtured a collective commitment to upholding their legacy.

Central to their strategy was the creation of a comprehensive estate plan, ensuring a seamless transfer of assets while minimizing potential conflicts and tax liabilities. The family's dedication to open dialogue facilitated discussions on financial matters, reinforcing shared aspirations and principles. Diversifying their assets across various classes played a crucial role in navigating economic fluctuations, bolstering resilience in their financial portfolio. Seeking guidance from financial planners and tax experts ensured that their strategies remained well-informed and adaptable. Additionally, the Johnsons embraced philanthropy, establishing a family foundation that not only made a positive impact on their community but also instilled a sense of purpose within the family. Teaching responsible wealth stewardship and regularly reviewing their financial plan completed their holistic approach to building a legacy that transcends material riches.

The Money Mindset

Chapter 5

Win-Win

Life's financial journey is a blend of expected victories and unforeseen hurdles, often termed as "tails." To navigate this uncertain terrain effectively, it's essential to construct a safety net that extends beyond standard planning – envision it as erecting a stronghold against unexpected storms.

Foremost, establish an emergency fund – your financial cushion designed to weather medical emergencies, unexpected job disruptions, or sudden home repairs. It serves as your buffer against life's unexpected twists and turns.

Yet, that's just the beginning. View insurance as your protective barrier, shielding you from significant setbacks. Whether it's health, life, or property insurance, having sufficient coverage mitigates the financial impact of unforeseen events. It functions as your safety net, ensuring you remain steady when life throws unexpected challenges your way.

Now, let's delve into investments – akin to cultivating a diverse garden. Diversification serves as your invaluable defense against market uncertainties. By spreading your investments across various assets and industries, you fortify your portfolio against downturns in any single sector. This strategic approach ensures that your overall investment remains robust, capable of withstanding unexpected market fluctuations.

Next, consider the ongoing learning curve as akin to adding new tools to your toolkit. Remaining relevant in today's dynamic job market isn't solely about the present; it's about fostering resilience for the future. Continuously expanding your knowledge base ensures adaptability, empowering you to pivot effectively when confronted with unforeseen challenges.

Legal and estate planning serve as the architectural blueprints for your legacy. Establishing a comprehensive plan guarantees that your assets are distributed according to your wishes. It's akin to providing your loved ones with a clear roadmap to navigate unforeseen events with minimal disruption and utmost clarity.

Let's delve into budgeting – not the rigid type, but a flexible approach. Contingency budgeting allocates funds specifically for unforeseen expenses or fluctuations in income. It's a pragmatic method of managing financial uncertainties without disrupting your overall financial plan.

Building robust networks is akin to assembling a supportive team. Your connections offer assistance during challenging times – whether through job referrals, emotional support, or shared resources. These relationships within your community and professional circles serve as your lifeline during unexpected circumstances.

Regular financial check-ups are akin to preventative care for your finances. By reviewing goals, evaluating debts, and ensuring your investments align with your objectives, you identify potential weaknesses. It's your proactive strategy for staying ahead of potential challenges.

Having an adaptable mindset and resilience serves as your mental fortitude. Life's twists and turns are inevitable, and the capacity to rebound from setbacks is invaluable. Resilience enables you to glean lessons from experiences and confront unforeseen hurdles with optimism and proactive problem-solving.

Furthermore, staying abreast of economic trends acts as your predictive tool. Economic fluctuations, geopolitical shifts, or changes within specific industries can have widespread repercussions. Continuously monitoring these trends empowers you to anticipate potential challenges and adapt your financial strategies accordingly.

Thus, preparing for financial uncertainties isn't merely about having a plan; it's about constructing a robust fortress, a resilient ecosystem capable of withstanding unexpected turbulence. It's your declaration of readiness to tackle whatever life throws your way.

Winning Strategies

Starting your journey towards financial success is akin to venturing into unknown territories – it requires a strategic approach to steer through both the currents of opportunity and the challenges ahead. To ensure a successful voyage, embrace these effective strategies, akin to a carefully drawn map rather than a rigid blueprint.

Define Your Destination: Imagine your financial aspirations as the guiding beacon, akin to the North Star, illuminating your path. Whether it involves purchasing a house, financing education, or ensuring a comfortable retirement, delineating clear goals offers clarity and a sense of purpose.

Craft Your Financial Compass: Consider your budget as a reliable navigational tool, much like a steadfast compass. Develop a thorough budget that mirrors your earnings, expenditures, and savings objectives. This not only helps you stay on track but also guarantees that your resources are directed toward your most important priorities.

Invest Strategically: Investing serves as the breeze propelling your financial journey forward. Formulate a savvy investment plan customized to match your risk tolerance and objectives. Broaden your portfolio to capture diverse financial opportunities and steer through the dynamic shifts of the market.

Build a Financial Lifeboat: Unforeseen challenges are bound to arise. Establishing an emergency fund acts as your financial safety net, ready to navigate through unexpected storms. Setting aside funds equivalent to three to six months of living expenses offers a comforting cushion against unforeseen circumstances.

Tame the Debt Dragon: Managing debts can feel like navigating turbulent waters. Focus on paying off high-interest debts first to smooth your financial journey. By adopting a disciplined approach to debt management, you take control of your finances and optimize your path forward.

Navigate Risks with Caution: Identify and assess potential risks as you navigate the financial waters. Implementing strategies to navigate around these risks ensures the safety of your financial vessel amid unforeseen challenges.

Embrace Adaptability: Consider adaptability as the navigation system aboard your financial vessel. Remain flexible in adjusting your strategies according to shifting winds, economic currents, or personal objectives. Embracing adaptability enables you to navigate unforeseen challenges with agility and confidence.

Keep Your Eyes on the Horizon: Achieving success is an ongoing journey, not a fixed destination. Keep your sights on the long term. Although immediate gains might seem enticing, prioritizing your overarching financial objectives enables you to navigate through shifting circumstances effectively.

Regularly Chart Your Course: Picture routinely inspecting your navigational tools. Perform regular evaluations of your financial well-being. Assess your objectives, scrutinize your investments, and adapt as the financial landscape shifts.

Leverage Modern Tools: In the contemporary era, technology serves as your guidepost. Embrace applications and digital platforms to simplify your financial voyage. Whether it's budgeting aids or investment applications, technology can enhance the efficiency of your financial navigation.

Celebrating Wins and Learning from Setbacks

The financial journey of life resembles a symphony, where both triumphs and trials compose the melody that guides us forward. Each achievement, whether it's reaching a savings milestone, navigating a successful investment, or conquering a financial challenge, warrants applause. These moments not only mark progress but also embody dedication and resilience. Equally significant are the setbacks, offering invaluable lessons in financial strategies, risk management, and personal fortitude. Rather than viewing obstacles as barriers, they present opportunities for growth and refinement. Reflecting on missteps, adjusting approaches, and assimilating the insights gained pave the way for a more enlightened and resilient financial future. Celebrating victories acknowledges effort and advancement, fueling motivation for the journey ahead. Learning from setbacks transforms hurdles into stepping stones, fostering a bedrock of wisdom that strengthens your financial trajectory. Together, these experiences harmonize, shaping a narrative of continuous growth and empowerment within your financial journey. Thus, cherish achievements, no matter how modest, and embrace setbacks as seeds of wisdom that blossom into a resilient and prosperous financial odyssey.

.

Chapter 6

Freedom

Financial freedom transcends mere numbers on a bank statement; it embodies a transformative journey imbued with empowerment, autonomy, and tranquility. It grants the liberty to shape life according to one's desires, making decisions driven by passion and purpose rather than financial constraints.

Visualize financial freedom as a meticulously crafted novel, each chapter unfolding a facet of this liberating odyssey. It commences with mindful spending – a deliberate approach to managing financial inflows and outflows. It's not solely about frugality but about conscientiously selecting options that resonate with personal values and aspirations. It entails discerning between essentials and desires, acknowledging that genuine wealth emanates from cherished experiences and moments of joy.

Saving assumes a pivotal role in this narrative. It transcends mere accumulation; it entails erecting a safety net, a shield against life's unpredictable twists and turns. The capacity to withstand adversities – whether a health crisis or sudden job loss – emerges as a hallmark of financial freedom. It entails fortifying the financial groundwork, ensuring that setbacks are temporary deviations rather than insurmountable obstacles.

Investing emerges as the central figure, driving the plot forward. It's not a gamble but a calculated negotiation between risk and reward. Prudent investing involves comprehending personal objectives, risk tolerance, and investment horizon. It epitomizes the journey toward wealth accumulation, harnessing financial resources to generate opportunities for future growth and fulfillment.

However, this narrative is not devoid of challenges. Financial freedom perceives setbacks as plot twists rather than conclusive tragedies. It involves learning from errors, adapting strategies, and regarding failures as pivotal moments toward a more enlightened financial future. Each setback serves as a character-building episode, an opportunity to refine approaches and fortify the journey.

Significantly, financial freedom is intertwined with the concept of time – the most invaluable resource. It entails gaining the freedom to allocate time according to personal desires and values. This isn't a race against time but a deliberate choice to cherish meaningful moments. Time becomes a currency invested in personal growth, meaningful relationships, and self-discovery.

The story of financial freedom also embodies a shift in mindset. It represents the transition from a scarcity mindset, where every expenditure feels like a loss, to an abundance mindset, where each financial decision is a step toward a richer life. It's about recognizing money as a tool, a means to an end rather than an end itself. Financial freedom isn't about pursuing wealth for its own sake but about pursuing a fulfilling life, where choices resonate with passions and values.

In essence, financial freedom orchestrates a symphony of fiscal prudence, intentional decisions, and a mindset that transcends numerical constraints. It's a journey toward a truly liberated existence, where individuals can sculpt their lives in harmony with their deepest aspirations. It's not solely about accumulating wealth but about crafting a life that reflects one's values, passions, and dreams. Financial freedom entails mastering the art of storytelling where money serves as an enabler, not a master, and each financial choice contributes to the masterpiece of a well-rounded life.

The Relationship Between Financial Freedom and Happiness

The interplay between financial freedom and happiness is intricate, intertwining the practicalities of security, the subtleties of mindset, and the depth of life experiences. At its essence, financial freedom lays a sturdy foundation for happiness by alleviating the pressures of survival and instilling a sense of security. It provides the reassurance that basic needs can be met without constant apprehension.

However, the narrative is far from straightforward. Once essential needs are fulfilled, the relationship between increased wealth and happiness becomes more nuanced. It's not about an incessant quest for more but about discovering the balance of "enough" – possessing adequate resources to lead a satisfying life. Studies suggest the fleeting nature of material pursuits, demonstrating how the pleasure derived from higher income tends to be transient.

Importantly, it's not merely about the figures in your bank account; it's about how you leverage your financial freedom. Happiness flourishes when financial resources are directed towards experiences, personal development, and giving back to others. It's the fulfillment found in meaningful endeavors and the warmth of nurturing connections, rather than the accumulation of possessions.

Mindset emerges as a pivotal element in this narrative. Deliberate and mindful financial management, coupled with appreciation for what one possesses, emerges as a potent force in shaping happiness. Steering clear of comparison and embracing one's unique journey contribute to a more contented life.

Nonetheless, it's crucial to acknowledge that financial freedom isn't a shield against life's adversities, nor does it guarantee perpetual happiness. Health, relationships, and a sense of purpose remain integral factors that influence overall well-being.

Crafting a Life Aligned with Personal Freedom

Creating a life in harmony with personal freedom is a creative endeavor that surpasses traditional routes and societal norms. It involves purposefully crafting a story that mirrors your beliefs, interests, and dreams, diverging from preconceived roles.

Central to this pursuit is the recognition that personal freedom extends beyond escaping external limitations; it also entails an inner emancipation. It encompasses the liberty to express your true self, embracing your individuality while shedding societal expectations that dictate conformity.

This journey entails a purposeful exploration of your values – the fundamental beliefs that define your priorities and aspirations. Identifying these values acts as a guiding light, steering your decisions and behaviors toward a life that reflects your innermost convictions.

Breaking away from societal expectations marks a courageous stride in this creative process. It involves recognizing that conventional norms may not align with your true identity. Personal freedom empowers you to redefine success according to your own standards, liberated from external pressures.

Mindful decision-making becomes a cornerstone of this endeavor. It involves intentionally allocating your time, energy, and resources. Each choice, regardless of its magnitude, contributes to the canvas of your existence. It's the distinction between living on autopilot and crafting a purposeful existence.

Simplification emerges as an art form in itself. Personal freedom often thrives in simplicity – in decluttering not only physical environments but also mental and emotional spaces. Letting go of what no longer serves your authentic self creates room for what truly matters.

Embracing personal freedom entails fostering a positive rapport with uncertainty. Life's path is inherently unpredictable, and personal freedom manifests in the capacity to navigate ambiguity with resilience and adaptability.

Interpersonal bonds hold significant sway in this cultivated existence. It involves nurturing connections that elevate, motivate, and resonate with your core values. Establishing a supportive community becomes foundational, serving as both a safety net and a wellspring of encouragement along your individual journey.

Furthermore, personal freedom is an ongoing journey rather than a fixed destination. It encourages continual self-exploration and growth. As you evolve and mature, so does the fabric of your crafted life. It's a vibrant tapestry in flux, not a static portrait.

The Money Mindset

Chapter 7

Hidden Prosperity

Embarking on a journey to explore wealth involves grasping a profound revelation: "The Unseen Dimensions of Wealth." In a society frequently fixated on conspicuous symbols of prosperity, this narrative urges us to look beyond the surface and unravel the complexities that constitute genuine abundance. It's an expedition that goes beyond the tangible and delves into the intangible, where the true richness of existence resides.

Pause for a moment to contemplate the invisible treasures that underpin authentic wealth. Optimal health emerges as an invaluable asset, often overshadowed by the pursuit of material wealth. The capacity to relish life's moments, engage in meaningful endeavors, and experience vitality constitutes an unseen wealth that transcends mere possessions.

Equally essential are the relationships we nurture. The unseen wealth of fulfilling connections, grounded in trust, affection, and shared experiences, holds immeasurable significance. These relationships enhance our lives, offering a support network that extends beyond material possessions, fostering a sense of belonging and emotional well-being.

The quest for knowledge represents another concealed dimension of wealth. The insights gleaned from life's experiences, the wisdom accumulated, and the perpetual quest for enlightenment all contribute to a form of wealth that transcends monetary value. It's the unseen reservoir of intellectual capital that fuels personal development and fortifies resilience in the face of life's trials.

Furthermore, there exists a richness in enriching the lives of others. Acts of kindness, generosity, and efforts to make a positive impact generate an intangible wealth that resonates far beyond individual boundaries. It's the immaterial currency of benevolence and constructive influence that serves as the bedrock of a thriving and interconnected society.

Recognizing the concealed facets of wealth prompts a reevaluation of our conception of prosperity. It entails shifting from a narrow fixation on material possessions to a broader, more holistic outlook. This journey encourages us to acknowledge that genuine wealth extends beyond what is visible, encompassing personal contentment, meaningful relationships, and the enduring legacy of positive contributions.

As we embark on this journey of discovery, we realize that the hidden dimensions of wealth are not distant or intangible; they are intricately integrated into the everyday moments of our existence. It's the joy found in cherished conversations with family and friends, the serenity of solitary contemplation, the wisdom acquired through varied encounters, and the uplifting influence we have on the lives of those around us. These elements form the intricate weave of a fulfilled and meaningful life.

Balancing Visibility and Privacy in Financial Matters

In the intricate landscape of financial management, achieving a balance between openness and confidentiality is akin to a delicate dance – a mindful endeavor to harmonize the sharing and safeguarding of financial information. Within the framework of Striking a Balance Between Transparency and Privacy in Financial Affairs, the decisions we make regarding what to disclose and what to keep private emerge as pivotal threads in the fabric of our financial health.

Transparency acts as a window into our financial realm, fostering trust and understanding. Engaging in open dialogues about financial objectives, shared responsibilities, and budgeting lays the groundwork for mutual comprehension in personal and professional relationships. It facilitates collaborative decision-making, promoting alignment in financial goals and reducing the potential for misunderstandings.

However, the pursuit of transparency must be balanced with the need for discretion. Certain aspects of our financial affairs warrant privacy. Whether it pertains to personal spending habits, intricate investment details, or confidential transactions, there are elements we opt to shield from public scrutiny. This guarded approach serves as a protective measure against unwelcome intrusions and upholds our autonomy over specific financial decisions.

The digital era introduces an added layer of intricacy to this delicate equilibrium. While online platforms offer unparalleled convenience, they also present potential threats to privacy. Upholding the security of personal data, leveraging secure communication channels, and exercising caution regarding our digital footprint emerge as essential practices for preserving financial confidentiality in the digital domain.

The decision to strike a balance between transparency and privacy is deeply individualized. It is influenced by personal comfort levels, cultural norms, and the dynamics of relationships. What we opt to disclose to a trusted financial advisor may differ from what we share with friends, family members, or colleagues. Respecting these boundaries is paramount in nurturing a healthy financial environment.

This equilibrium transcends mere information protection; it embodies empowerment. It entails exercising discernment in the narratives we choose to divulge and comprehending the potential ramifications of financial disclosures. It signifies an acknowledgment that privacy serves not only as a shield but also as a tool enabling intentional curation of our financial narrative.

In a realm where conversations about finances vacillate between secrecy and openness, achieving this equilibrium becomes a skillful practice. It involves defining boundaries, grasping the consequences of financial disclosures, and determining opportune moments for sharing, fostering mutual advantage. This nuanced interplay acknowledges that financial health extends beyond numerical figures; it revolves around shaping a story that reflects individual values, cultivates trust, and empowers autonomy in steering our distinct financial path.

The Value of Discretion

This feels akin to intentionally stepping away from the glaring spotlight of wealth. It's not about concealment, but rather about selecting the timing and manner in which we disclose the intricate facets of our financial journey. Discretion serves as a trusted guide, helping us shape a narrative where the true essence of prosperity transcends public scrutiny.

In this context, discretion isn't synonymous with secrecy; it's a deliberate choice to thoughtfully manage the visibility of our wealth. It acknowledges that certain aspects of affluence are best appreciated beyond the constant gaze of the public. This mindful privacy acts as a shield against undesired attention, granting us control over the narratives surrounding our financial decisions.

At its essence, discretion embodies the understanding that wealth is a deeply individual journey, filled with subtleties best appreciated in moments of reflection. It entails safeguarding the intimacy of financial decisions, shielding them from external scrutiny, and embracing a sense of empowerment over our choices.

This discreet approach isn't a retreat from engagement with the world, but rather a strategic maneuver, particularly in a society often swayed by external appearances. It enables us to navigate our financial path with discernment, steering clear of pitfalls like undue influence or unwelcome expectations. By keeping the value of wealth understated, we underscore the importance of personal satisfaction, experiences, and meaningful contributions over ostentatious displays.

Beyond a mere strategic maneuver, discretion embodies a humble posture amidst abundance. It authentically recognizes that true wealth isn't measured by flashy exhibitions but by its impact on our lives and the lives of those around us. This unassuming approach serves as a contrast to the prevailing culture of extravagance, urging us to cultivate a more grounded and genuine connection with prosperity.

In an era where our lives are constantly showcased on social media and digital platforms, the importance of discretion becomes even more pronounced. It acts as a shield against the pressures of comparison and the potential drawbacks of excessive visibility. By embracing discretion, we can navigate our financial path with elegance and mindfulness, liberated from the confines of external expectations.

The Money Mindset

Chapter 8

Error, Growth, and the True Cost of Choices

Setting out on the financial voyage requires acknowledging that errors are not deviations but rather indispensable markers for advancement. Advocating for an Openness to Financial Mistakes and Gaining Wisdom from Errors calls for a shift in mindset, recognizing that misjudgments are intrinsic to the quest for financial acumen.

Financial missteps, whether minor miscalculations or major setbacks, are reframed not as defeats but as chances to hone one's strategy. This outlook urges individuals to view these deviations as pivotal instances for individual growth and fortitude enhancement.

Establishing an environment that permits financial errors isn't a sanction of irresponsibility but a practical recognition that, in the pursuit of financial expertise, occasional divergences may arise. This acceptance nurtures a setting where trial and error is appreciated, creativity is embraced, and insights are gleaned from every financial choice.

Extracting lessons from financial missteps entails a reflective journey. Grasping the context, actions, or choices that contributed to the misstep is crucial. By unraveling these fundamental elements, individuals acquire understanding that empowers them to preemptively adopt measures to alleviate comparable risks down the road.

Additionally, this viewpoint underscores the significance of seeking guidance and drawing lessons from the experiences of others. Whether through mentorship, financial literacy programs, or shared stories, leveraging external insights offers valuable perspectives that enrich a more knowledgeable and adaptable financial mindset.

Fundamentally, Embracing Space for Financial Mistakes and Learning from Errors presents a narrative that normalizes occasional missteps within the financial journey. It prompts individuals to perceive mistakes as integral to their progress, each one contributing to personal and financial development. This approach emboldens individuals to navigate their financial path with curiosity, resilience, and an ongoing dedication to self-improvement, recognizing that errors are not impediments but rather essential elements along the journey to financial enlightenment.

Embracing Change

Venturing into the intersection of personal development and financial perspectives is akin to entering a multifaceted tapestry of self-exploration. It entails delving into the intricate interplay between individual growth and the transformation of our approach to money.

Personal development serves as a subtle yet potent catalyst, fundamentally reshaping our perception of wealth. As we mature emotionally, intellectually, and spiritually, our relationship with finances experiences a profound evolution. This transcends mere monetary transactions; it celebrates a form of prosperity that extends beyond financial metrics, embracing the depth of self-discovery and the refinement of our fundamental principles.

A notable transition in this journey involves a shift from materialistic pursuits towards a more holistic conception of prosperity. As personal growth unfolds, the allure of conspicuous consumption often gives way to a deeper appreciation for experiences, meaningful connections, and contributions to a higher purpose. The focus transitions from amassing material possessions to cultivating a life that is rich in fulfillment and aligned with a sense of purpose.

Equally notable is the heightened sense of financial accountability fostered by personal growth. As we develop emotionally and gain deeper insights into our values, there emerges a natural inclination to harmonize our financial decisions with these newfound understandings. This transition prompts a more deliberate approach to spending, saving, and investing, prioritizing choices that resonate authentically with our core selves.

This narrative also encompasses resilience in the face of financial adversities. Personal growth equips us with the emotional maturity to navigate setbacks with composure. Challenges cease to be mere obstacles; they become opportunities for growth, shifting the storyline from mere survival to flourishing amidst financial uncertainties.

In the realm of How Personal Growth Influences Financial Perspectives, it acknowledges that financial literacy transcends numerical proficiency; it encompasses emotional intelligence and self-awareness. It entails comprehending the motives guiding our financial choices, recognizing recurring patterns, and actively shaping a financial narrative that aligns with our personal growth aspirations.

The Real Cost of "Free"

Embarking on the exploration of the intricate realm of financial decisions within the context of "Understanding Hidden Costs in Financial Choices" feels akin to unveiling a well-guarded secret. It's a journey that urges us to scrutinize the alluring promise of "free" and unravel the concealed expenses often lurking behind seemingly costless options.

Let's commence by debunking the illusion of "free." It's a captivating term that tempts us to try out a new app, sample a subscription at no initial charge, or enroll in a service without an immediate monetary transaction. However, this expedition compels us to pose a critical inquiry: What lies beneath the facade of this apparent generosity? It's an opportunity to peel back the layers and recognize that, more often than not, there's a hidden price waiting to be revealed.

Delving deeper than just tangible expenses, the exploration ventures into the psychological realm of "free." There's an inherent allure in acquiring something without any monetary outlay, and this initial zero-cost appeal can obscure our judgment. It's like being under a spell that leads us to overlook potential long-term consequences. Understanding this psychological dynamic empowers us to make decisions with clarity, recognizing the implicit value exchange that accompanies seemingly costless offerings.

But our exploration doesn't end there; let's illuminate the ripple effects of hidden costs. Choices that appear to be free of charge often entail broader ramifications. It might entail relinquishing personal data, investing more time than initially anticipated, or unintentionally committing to future financial obligations. This narrative urges us to look beyond the immediate transaction, acknowledging the subtleties that can shape our financial landscape.

At the core of this exploration lies a plea to adopt a proactive mindset. Armed with an understanding of hidden costs, we gain the ability to approach decision-making with discernment. It involves looking beyond the surface, foreseeing potential repercussions, and ensuring our choices are in line with our long-term financial objectives. This proactive approach shifts us from passive recipients of the allure of freebies to astute decision-makers navigating the complex landscape of financial choices.

Essentially, delving into "The True Expense of 'Free'" is a journey into the art of financial decision-making. It encourages us to peer beyond the superficial appeal of zero-cost offerings and recognize the intricate web of consequences that accompany them. It urges us to embrace a mindset that acknowledges the genuine cost of apparently costless choices, enabling us to traverse the financial terrain with clarity, foresight, and a deep awareness of the concealed factors intertwined with our decisions. It's not solely about the monetary aspect; it's about comprehending the narratives woven by our financial choices and making decisions that align with the stories we aspire to craft for our future selves.

Chapter 9

Financial Resilience: Save, Reason, Adapt

Saving money transcends mere financial practice; it stands as a pillar of personal well-being that reverberates across various facets of our lives. Fundamentally, saving acts as a safety cushion, providing a vital buffer against the unexpected twists of life. Whether faced with a sudden medical bill or an unanticipated car repair, having savings at hand instills a sense of security, ensuring we can navigate these hurdles without plunging into financial chaos.

Yet, saving goes beyond mere crisis management; it serves as a key to unlocking our aspirations. Whether our ambitions involve homeownership, entrepreneurial ventures, or educational pursuits, having a reservoir of savings empowers us to translate dreams into reality. Savings serve as the propellant driving us toward our objectives, bridging the gap between distant aspirations and tangible achievements.

Saving cultivates financial discipline in our day-to-day lives, prompting mindful spending and living within our means. By regularly allocating a portion of our income to savings, we establish a routine of deliberate financial decision-making, influencing our approach to budgeting, investing, and overall financial management.

Moreover, the impact of saving extends to wealth accumulation. Through consistent saving practices and prudent investment strategies, we harness the potential of compound interest. Over time, our savings not only accrue but also generate returns, leading to a compounding effect that significantly boosts our wealth. This long-term perspective lays the groundwork for financial security and autonomy in the future.

Above and beyond mere numerical value, maintaining savings cultivates a feeling of financial independence and tranquility. It diminishes dependence on credit and debt, alleviating the anxiety often associated with financial insecurity. The assurance of having a financial buffer instills a sense of assurance and enables us to make well-considered and purposeful choices regarding our finances.

Taking a broader perspective, a populace characterized by a shared inclination toward saving fosters economic stability. Individual savings serve as a sturdy base that bolsters the collective financial well-being of societies and nations. This fosters a more resilient community capable of weathering economic downturns and uncertainties with greater ease.

Fundamentally, saving transcends mere monetary value, encompassing a lifestyle and mindset that molds a more secure, prosperous, and fulfilling future. Therefore, when you allocate a portion of your income to savings, recognize that you're not merely hoarding money; rather, you're investing in your aspirations, nurturing discipline, and contributing to a more stable and resilient global community.

Shifting our attention to the cultivation of financial reserves, this endeavor extends beyond the simple act of squirreling away funds; it resembles constructing a robust fortress to safeguard your economic well-being. Picture it as a toolkit brimming with pragmatic strategies that surpass routine saving practices, designed to bolster your financial security against life's uncertainties.

A pivotal aspect of this approach involves establishing achievable savings targets. This isn't a one-size-fits-all proposition; it entails comprehending your unique financial landscape and devising objectives that align with your ambitions. Whether it involves creating an emergency fund, accumulating a down payment, or assembling resources for future opportunities, these objectives serve as guiding beacons, directing your savings journey with clarity and purpose.

Discipline serves as a cornerstone in this financial voyage. Cultivating a disciplined savings regimen resembles tending to a flourishing garden. Consistency is paramount, and this routine should harmonize with your income structure. Whether it entails a fixed percentage or a designated sum each month, this regularity imbues saving with a steadfast rhythm, progressively nurturing the financial reserves that will serve as your economic fortress.

Striking a balance between reason and rationality in financial choices is another pivotal aspect. Rationality adheres strictly to logic, whereas being reasonable acknowledges the human element in decision-making. This necessitates finding an equilibrium — being rational enough to make well-informed decisions while allowing space for the reasonable need to adapt to life's unpredictabilities.

Surprises are inevitable on the financial path, and the strategy here is to embrace them with adaptability. Your financial blueprint isn't a static document; rather, it's a dynamic entity that evolves alongside your life. Whether presented with a sudden expense or an unforeseen windfall, adaptability enables you to recalibrate your savings strategy, ensuring it remains aligned with your evolving circumstances.

Diversification isn't confined to investment portfolios; it extends to the construction of financial reserves as well. Explore diverse savings avenues aligned with your objectives and risk tolerance. While a conventional savings account provides security for emergencies, contemplate investments for longer-term goals. Diversifying your savings strategy not only bolsters your financial resilience but also unlocks opportunities for potential growth.

Automation emerges as a valuable tool. Establish automated transfers to your savings account, guaranteeing that a portion of your income is allocated to reserves before other expenditures. Automation eliminates the need for continual manual interventions, streamlining the process and ensuring consistency.

When unexpected financial windfalls, such as bonuses or unexpected gains, come your way, utilize them strategically. Rather than viewing them as a reason for immediate splurging, allocate a portion to your reserves. This ensures that these financial windfalls contribute to your long-term stability rather than dissipating unnoticed.

Peek ahead with foresight. Predict forthcoming expenses, whether they're scheduled occurrences or potential emergencies. Gaining a clear understanding of what's on the horizon enables you to adjust your savings approach accordingly, averting disruptions to your financial stability from these future events.

Moreover, never cease to expand your knowledge of personal finance. Keep yourself updated on potential investment prospects, optimal savings avenues, and financial trends. Arming yourself with information not only enhances your decision-making abilities but also positions you to adapt to evolving financial landscapes.

Fundamentally, constructing financial reserves constitutes a dynamic journey, not a fixed endpoint. It involves nurturing a mindset and lifestyle that prioritize your financial well-being, enabling you to confront the unexpected with assurance and sculpt a secure and prosperous future.

Navigating Financial Decisions

In navigating financial decisions, there's often a delicate balance between reason and rationality. Rather than strictly adhering to logic and numerical calculations, this journey encourages us to acknowledge the human aspect that influences our decisions. It's an exploration of those instances where being sensible prevails over adhering strictly to rationality.

Practically speaking, rationality may require steadfast adherence to a predetermined plan or budget. While this approach has its benefits, being sensible injects a vital element of empathy and adaptability into the equation. It recognizes that the financial journey of life isn't always a straightforward calculation but rather a nuanced interplay of emotions, circumstances, and unexpected variables.

For instance, consider the process of budgeting. A purely rational approach might insist on strict adherence to the budget, allocating fixed amounts to various categories without any flexibility. However, being sensible allows for adjustments based on real-life situations. It acknowledges that unforeseen expenses or opportunities may arise, and adapting the budget to accommodate these changes isn't a sign of failure but a pragmatic response.

In the domain of investments, being sensible acknowledges that the market doesn't always operate in a rational or predictable manner. While a rational approach might advocate for a meticulously calculated strategy, being sensible allows for a nuanced comprehension of market dynamics, recognizing the emotional facets and market sentiment.

This sensible mindset also applies to personal goals and aspirations. It acknowledges life's fluidity, understanding that priorities can evolve over time. Whereas a strictly rational approach might demand steadfast commitment to predetermined financial goals, being sensible permits adjustments based on changing circumstances and personal development.

When confronted with financial setbacks or unexpected opportunities, being sensible serves as a beacon of practical wisdom. It promotes a deliberate evaluation of the situation, considering the logical aspects alongside the emotional and contextual factors. This approach cultivates resilience and the capacity to navigate financial decisions with a broader perspective.

The exploration of financial decision-making where practicality surpasses strict logic invites us to embrace the intricacies of human experiences in handling finances. It recognizes that financial choices often exist in shades of gray, and incorporating a dose of practicality enriches the texture and flexibility of our economic decisions. As we navigate the intricacies of personal finance, prioritizing reasonableness becomes a guiding ethos, enabling us to make well-informed decisions while remaining sensitive to the nuanced dynamics of our financial path.

Adapting to the Unpredictable

Life has a tendency to present unforeseen challenges, particularly in the realm of our finances. Embracing the unforeseen and adjusting to the unpredictable introduces a fluid element to our financial path.

Within the realm of personal finance, surprises encompass a spectrum, ranging from unwelcome occurrences such as sudden car repairs or unforeseen medical expenses to more pleasant occurrences like unexpected bonuses or inheritances. Rather than regarding these fluctuations as disturbances, the approach is to greet them with flexibility and adaptability.

When confronted with unforeseen costs, the strategy isn't to panic but to acknowledge them as natural facets of life. It entails modifying our financial strategy to accommodate these unexpected shifts, whether it means accessing emergency funds or reevaluating budget allocations.

Windfalls, those unforeseen financial windfalls, demand a distinct form of adaptability. Instead of yielding to the allure of immediate gratification, embracing these unexpected blessings requires making deliberate choices about how they can support long-term financial objectives, such as bolstering reserves or investing for the future.

Market fluctuations are yet another dimension of financial uncertainty. Rather than fearing or opposing these shifts, welcoming surprises in the shape of economic changes entails adapting investment approaches. It accepts that markets are inherently volatile, and being adaptable is crucial for managing the fluctuations effectively. Embracing surprises goes beyond mere reaction; it involves consciously integrating flexibility into our financial plans. It acknowledges life's fluidity, and our financial tactics should mirror this ever-changing nature. This mindset cultivates resilience, enabling us to confront uncertainties with a composed outlook.

Furthermore, surprises aren't solely financial obstacles; they present chances for development. Embracing the unforeseen entails seizing these chances, learning from unexpected circumstances, and using them to refine our financial strategies. It's about transforming surprises into building blocks for enhanced financial acumen and readiness.

Fundamentally, the journey of accepting surprises and adjusting to the unpredictable acknowledges that our financial journey isn't linear but rather a winding path with twists and turns. It urges us to foster a mentality that embraces the unexpected, converting surprises into valuable insights and opportunities for financial advancement. As we navigate life's uncertainties, this adaptability emerges as a guiding principle, ensuring that our financial plans remain resilient and robust in the face of whatever surprises arise.

Chapter 10

Bridging Beliefs: The Heart of Financial Connections

The fusion of money and relationships reveals a nuanced network of interpersonal interactions that deeply influence the trajectory of partnerships. Maneuvering through the complexities of intertwining relationships and finances demands a careful equilibrium, transparent dialogue, and a mutual outlook for the future.

Financial discussions frequently serve as a gauge for the strength of a relationship. It goes beyond mere figures, encompassing shared principles, objectives, and the capacity to confront obstacles as a team. Establishing an environment of open and sincere communication becomes essential, fostering a space where both individuals feel acknowledged, comprehended, and valued.

Varying financial behaviors and perspectives often lead to friction, underscoring the importance of establishing mutual understanding. Aligning on financial objectives, spending patterns, and future aspirations lays the groundwork for financial unity. Rather than eliminating individual disparities, the focus is on discovering a cooperative strategy that honors each person's principles and convictions.

Transparency serves as a fundamental element in navigating the interpersonal dynamics of finance. Candid discussions about earnings, debts, and monetary objectives foster trust. Concealing financial secrets or burdens can strain relationships, underscoring the necessity of fostering an environment where both partners feel at ease discussing financial affairs.

Establishing clear boundaries is crucial for managing financial obligations within a relationship. Whether it involves dividing expenses, establishing joint accounts, or preserving individual financial independence, clarifying roles and expectations is key to mitigating potential conflicts. This transparency provides a structured approach to decision-making and minimizes uncertainty.

Emotions frequently come into play in financial matters, and it's important to acknowledge the emotional dimension of these discussions. Empathy is vital - comprehending each other's viewpoints and recognizing the emotional significance of financial choices cultivates a supportive atmosphere.

During periods of financial difficulty, the strength of a relationship undergoes testing. Confronting challenges together, whether they stem from job loss, unforeseen expenses, or setbacks, strengthens the resilience of the partnership. It presents an opportunity for mutual assistance, problem-solving, and demonstrating dedication to overcoming obstacles as a unified team.

Financial planning as a couple encompasses not just immediate objectives but also long-term dreams. Harmonizing aspirations for significant life milestones, such as buying a home, starting a family, or retirement, ensures both partners are in sync. Regular assessments of financial progress and adjustments to plans foster a collective sense of achievement and purpose.

Finally, the interplay between finances and relationships is an ongoing process. As life progresses, financial situations evolve. Consistent communication and periodic review of financial objectives become essential in adjusting to shifts, sustaining a robust financial partnership, and fostering a relationship that matures alongside shared financial stability.

In essence, the interaction between relationships and finances is a dynamic voyage necessitating mutual comprehension, transparency, and a cooperative mindset. By recognizing the complexities of this intersection, couples can establish a bedrock of trust, tackle challenges collectively, and craft a joint financial story that reinforces the bonds of their partnership.

Navigating Trust

In the complex realm of financial choices, trust emerges as a pivotal factor directing our trajectory forward. It transcends mere transactions; it embodies a set of beliefs profoundly impacting our approach to and traversal of different facets of our financial path.

Fundamentally, financial trust revolves around placing confidence in the dependability and honesty of those implicated – whether it's a significant other, financial planner, or business partner. This conviction forms the cornerstone of our decision-making, guiding everything from joint investments to managing financial obligations in tandem.

Trust and open communication go hand in hand. It flourishes in an atmosphere where individuals freely disclose the financial dimensions of their lives, conversing about objectives, obstacles, and ambiguities. It transcends mere figures; it involves being candid and open about our financial circumstances.

In interpersonal connections, trust integrates into mutual financial obligations. Whether it entails combining finances, making joint acquisitions, or confronting financial hurdles jointly, trust serves as the glue that unites these choices. It embodies the belief that each party is acting in the partnership's best interest.

This trust transcends personal connections and extends into the professional arena, particularly when seeking financial guidance or engaging in business ventures. Having faith in the competence and ethical standards of financial advisors, business associates, or collaborators becomes essential, impacting choices related to investments and financial strategies.

Our individual belief systems also significantly influence trust formation. Cultural, familial, or personal beliefs regarding money shape our approach to financial matters. Placing trust in decisions that resonate with our fundamental beliefs instills confidence in the chosen financial path.

Consistency plays a vital role in establishing and preserving trust. Consistent fulfillment of financial obligations, adherence to agreements, and demonstration of ethical behavior over time reinforce the underlying belief that guides financial decisions. Conversely, inconsistency or breaches of trust can undermine this foundation.

Striking a harmonious balance between independence and cooperation is vital when navigating trust. While preserving individual financial autonomy holds significance, there exists a mutual understanding that each partner or collaborator can contribute responsibly to shared financial objectives. This equilibrium safeguards trust without compromising individuals' financial sovereignty.

Managing trust in financial matters constitutes an ongoing process. Regular evaluations, reevaluations, and adaptations in light of life's fluctuations contribute to the sustainability of trust. This fluid approach acknowledges that trust, akin to any facet of relationships, demands consistent care and cultivation.

Building Financial Understanding in Relationships

Developing financial comprehension within a relationship resembles embarking on a collaborative journey, where communication, mutual objectives, and a dedication to addressing financial affairs collectively serve as the guiding principles.

Effective communication lies at the core of financial comprehension. It involves establishing an environment where both partners feel at ease discussing various money matters – spanning from income to spending patterns and future financial ambitions. Regular check-ins serve as platforms for aligning viewpoints, ensuring that each partner's input is heard and respected throughout the financial decision-making process.

Establishing mutual financial goals injects a sense of purpose into the journey. Whether it entails saving for a dream vacation, a home, or planning for retirement, having common objectives fosters a sense of togetherness. These goals serve as guiding stars, shaping financial choices and reinforcing the notion that both partners are steering towards a shared future.

Mutual education about individual financial viewpoints is a fundamental component of fostering comprehension. This entails exchanging personal experiences, beliefs, and attitudes regarding money. Delving into the reasoning behind financial decisions fosters empathy and bridges gaps in financial understanding.

Establishing a joint budget is a pragmatic step towards financial openness. It provides a transparent overview of the financial terrain, encompassing income, expenditures, and savings. Co-managing a budget not only promotes transparency but also cultivates a shared sense of accountability in making prudent financial decisions.

Confronting financial obstacles collectively reinforces the bond of comprehension. Life presents unexpected hurdles, and unforeseen events can influence financial stability. Tackling these challenges as a unit nurtures resilience and enhances insight into each other's methods of financial management and problem-solving.

Maintaining a balance between individual financial independence and shared objectives is essential. While collaborative financial planning holds significance, allowing space for personal financial preferences ensures that both partners retain a sense of ownership and autonomy in overseeing their finances.

Nurturing a mindset of continuous learning in finance is an ongoing endeavor. Participating in financial workshops, reading books jointly, or consulting with experts enriches financial literacy and constructs a common pool of knowledge. This educational voyage underscores the notion that financial comprehension is an ongoing journey of evolution and advancement.

Marking financial milestones together solidifies the positive facets of financial cooperation. Whether it involves clearing a debt, attaining a savings target, or reaching a noteworthy financial achievement, recognizing these triumphs reinforces the feeling of shared success and promotes sustained financial collaboration.

It's crucial to regularly review and adjust financial plans. As life progresses, financial situations change. Remaining flexible and open to modifying strategies ensures that financial comprehension stays pertinent and adaptable to life's evolving dynamics.

Conclusion

As we near the end of "The Money Mindset," let's ponder the transformative voyage we've shared. In our exploration of the intricate interplay between finances and aspirations, we've delved into the profound psychology behind money, uncovering enduring insights about wealth, greed, and fulfillment. From navigating the fine line between chance and uncertainty to deciphering the powerful impact of compound interest on our financial paths, each chapter has been a building block toward a richer comprehension of the complex fabric of our monetary existence.

We've discovered that achieving wealth is merely the starting point; maintaining it requires distinct abilities and a steadfast dedication to financial stability. Scenarios where success is assured have emphasized the significance of readiness for unforeseen circumstances. Through Oliver's narrative, we observed the dangers of extravagance and the outcomes of seeking validation through material possessions. His story resonates throughout the book, serving as both a warning and a poignant reflection that our relationship with money goes beyond intellect and relies on our capacity to embrace humility and careful judgment.

"The Money Mindset" invites us to confront the notion of perpetual scarcity and liberate ourselves from the grip of consumerism. It encourages us to foster satisfaction, leverage the benefits of compounding, and approach risks with discernment. In our pursuit of enduring prosperity, we examined the intricate balance between planning and chance, acknowledging the significant contributions of both in shaping our financial stories.

As we wrap up this voyage, the focus lies not only on financial acumen but also on nurturing a mindset rooted in action. These pages have transformed into a guide for reshaping our attitudes towards money, stressing that success isn't merely about knowledge but about our behaviors and choices.

As you finish this book, dear reader, allow its lessons to resonate within you. Understand that handling money is more than just a skill; it's a form of art woven into the fabric of our existence. May you take with you the insights gathered from these pages, paving the way towards financial independence, satisfaction, and a mindset that surpasses the fleeting changes of the market.

The Money Mindset

Leaving a Review

Dear Reader,

I hope this message reaches you well. I deeply appreciate your decision to explore the contents of this book. Our shared journey has been remarkable, and my sincere wish is that you found the book informative and valuable.

As a writer, your feedback means a lot to me. I would greatly appreciate it if you could take a moment to share your thoughts and impressions by leaving a review on the platform where you acquired the book.

Your review is not only valuable feedback for me but also assists other readers in finding the book, enabling them to gauge its relevance to their preferences. Whether you provide a brief summary or a detailed reflection, your honest feedback is highly appreciated. Thank you for joining me on this journey through literature. I look forward to hearing your thoughts and sincerely appreciate the time and thoughtfulness you dedicate to it.

Warm regards,
Lane J. Taylor

www.ingramcontent.com/pod-product-compliance
Lightning Source LLC
Chambersburg PA
CBHW071045290526
45795CB00004B/1332